THE CARDINALS FAN'S
LITTLE BOOK OF WISDOM

THE CARDINALS FAN'S
LITTLE BOOK OF WISDOM
101 Truths...Learned The Hard Way

by Rob Rains

DIAMOND COMMUNICATIONS
An Imprint of The Rowman & Littlefield Publishing Group

Lanham • South Bend • New York • Toronto • Plymouth, UK

THE CARDINALS FAN'S LITTLE BOOK OF WISDOM
Copyright © 1994, 2002 by Rob Rains

Published by Diamond Communications
An imprint of The Rowman & Littlefield Publishing Group, Inc.
4501 Forbes Boulevard, Suite 200, Lanham, Maryland 20706

Distributed by NATIONAL BOOK NETWORK

The previous edition of this book was cataloged
by the Library of Congress as follows:

Rains, Rob.
The Cardinals fan's little book of wisdom : 101 truths—learned the hard
way / by Rob Rains.   p. cm.   1. St. Louis Cardinals (Baseball team)—
Humor.   2. St. Louis Cardinals (Baseball team)—Miscellanea.   I. Title.
GV875.S74R35 1994   796.357 '64'09778660207—dc20   94-23542   CIP
ISBN 1-888698-49-7 (pbk. : alk. paper)

Manufactured in the United States of America.

The scene was a third-grade classroom in Springfield, Missouri, where an eight-year-old youngster was finding it hard to concentrate—his beloved Cardinals were playing the Yankees in the World Series that afternoon.

Knowing his teacher wasn't a baseball fan, the wily student pulled one of the time-honored stunts out of the bag—he suddenly announced he was ill and had to go home. The teacher sent the pupil to the office, where his mother was called, and she dutifully reported to take him home.

Ah, the kid thought, there's the couch and the television. The game is about to start…this is going to be perfect, if the Cardinals could only find a way to win.

I was the kid, of course, and I already knew on that October day in 1964 that my love affair with the Cardinals was going to grow. Ken Boyer was my hero, and I spent many an afternoon and early evening in the backyard pretending to be Boyer while the voices of Jack Buck and Harry Caray brought the games to life.

My mother knew how much I cared about baseball and the Cardinals, but she also was a teacher and librarian. And when she found out I had faked being sick for the sole purpose of coming home to watch the game, my bubble was burst. Off to bed I went, banned not only from watching the game but also from listening to it on the radio.

I probably cried a lot that day—my memory of that has faded. What I am sure of is that was the day I decided what I wanted to be when I grew up—a sports-writer, covering the Cardinals, where it would be my job to watch the team play.

Some kids don't ever get to live their dreams, but I did. Those third-grade tears dried, and the Cardinals have since played in five World Series, and I had the fortune of covering three of them in my job as a reporter, first for *United Press International* and then for the *St. Louis Globe-Democrat*.

The Cardinals, I found out, had the same effect on a lot of other people throughout the Midwest as they had on me. When they won, your food tasted a little better and the sun looked a little brighter. When they lost, the entire day wasn't the same.

As I learned about the history of the franchise and the players who made it legendary, I knew the Cardinals were unique in sports. The list of Hall-of-Famers who starred over the years is long, topped by Stan Musial.

There also is a virtual endless list of fans who have passed their love of the Cardinals down to their children, and their children's children. I am proud to say my two boys, B.J. and Mike, are included in that group.

My oldest son entered the third grade this fall. He may love baseball even more than I did at his age. There is one difference, however. He can't fake being sick to come home to watch the World Series, because the games aren't played in the daytime anymore. The reason he doesn't watch all of the games is that they end too late at night, but that's a story for another time and place.

It might surprise my mom as well, but if he tried it and the game was on—I probably wouldn't let him watch it either. That's wisdom, gained 30 years later.

—*Rob Rains,*
September 1994

ABOUT THE AUTHOR

Rob Rains has been a staff writer for *USA Today Baseball Weekly* since the newspaper's inception in 1991. Prior to that, he was a reporter for *United Press International,* the *St. Louis Globe-Democrat,* and a freelance writer.

Rains also is the author of *Wizard: the Autobiography of Ozzie Smith* and *The St. Louis Cardinals' 100th Anniversary History.*

He lives with his wife and two sons in St. Louis, Missouri.

This book is dedicated to Bud Selig,
Richard Ravitch, and Donald Fehr,
who gave us a reason to
remember baseball the way
it used to be.

If you need to know how to endure the winter, consult the Rajah.

"People ask me what I do in winter when there's no baseball. I'll tell you what I do. I stare out the window and wait for spring."—Rogers Hornsby

Sometimes the least effective way is the only way.

"The way to catch a knuckleball is to wait until it stops rolling and then pick it up."—Bob Uecker

61 is a lucky number.

Mark McGwire's 61st homer in 1998, which tied Roger Maris'
single-season record, came at Busch Stadium on September 7,
with his father, John, sitting in the stands—
celebrating his 61st birthday.

All things considered, winning is better.

"When we lost, I couldn't sleep at night. When we win, I can't sleep at night. But when you win, you wake up feeling better."—Joe Torre

Sometimes it pays to leave the playing to others.

"Baseball has been very good to me since
I quit trying to play it."—Whitey Herzog

Speed isn't everything.

"I throw the ball 92 miles per hour, but they hit it back just as hard." —pitcher Joaquin Andujar

No situation is without a way to overcome the odds.

"When a pitcher's throwing a spitball, don't complain.
Just hit the dry side, like I do."—Stan Musial

A hitter, not a pitcher

In high school, some people were predicting Bud Smith might be
a major-league prospect after breaking Nomar Garciappara's
school records for batting average and RBI and tying his
home-run mark. Smith did not break any of major
leaguer Dennis Lamp's school records.

Leave some things to others.

"When I hit a ball, I want someone else to go
chase it."—Rogers Hornsby on why he didn't play golf

Know when to say "when."

"When I gave up a grand slam to Pete LaCock, I knew it was time to quit."—Bob Gibson

Home runs or bust.

Through the end of the 2001 season, Keith McDonald had three career hits in the major leagues for the Cardinals, and all were home runs. McDonald became only the second player in major league history to homer in his first two at-bats in the majors in 2000, joining Bob Nieman of the St. Louis Browns, who did it in 1951.

Sometimes you can help most by doing the least.

"I made a major contribution to the Cardinals'
pennant drive in 1964. I got hepatitis."—Bob Uecker

Read the card.

Ozzie Smith learned he was just 40 hits away from 2,000 hits for his career by reading the back of his baseball card. A friend had told him the statistic, and when Smith didn't believe him, he was told "Read the back of your baseball card."

Know how to position yourself for posterity.

"Always stand in the middle when you're having a group picture taken because that way they can't cut you out of it."—Stan Musial

Predicting the future

In Mark McGwire's first official Little League at-bat,
when he was 10 years old, he hit a home run.

Learn how to read the signs of success.

"There is no greater pleasure in the world than walking up to the plate with men on base and knowing that you are feared."—Ted Simmons

Keep it simple.

"The dumber a pitcher is, the better. When he gets smart and begins to experiment with a lot of different pitches, he's in trouble. All I ever had was a fastball, a curve, and a changeup. And I did pretty good."—Dizzy Dean

It's better than bleeding blue.

"When the baseball season starts in St. Louis, they bleed
(Cardinal) red. Everybody told me I would love St. Louis,
and no wonder." —Mark McGwire

Focus on the essentials.

"St. Louis is baseball All-American style. Not like Philly, not like New York, not like anywhere else. In St. Louis, the fans care about the game…they talked strategy, the hit-and-run, the squeeze play, the defensive alignment. The fans didn't care about off-field controversies."—Richie Allen

Always give simple instructions.

"You wait for a strike. Then you pound
the heck out of it."—Stan Musial

21

Ask yourself whether the latest is really the greatest.

"A great catch is like watching girls go by—the last one you see is always the prettiest."—Bob Gibson

Believe that you can— then do it.

"I'll tell you with my head that I'm going to steal second base. You know I'm going to, but there's nothing you can do to stop it."—Lou Brock

Luck often follows ability.

"Bob Gibson is the luckiest pitcher I've ever seen.
He always pitches on the day the other team
doesn't score any runs."—Tim McCarver

Sometimes use a verbal curve to fan your friend.

"The only thing you know about pitching is that you can't hit it."—Bob Gibson to Tim McCarver

Understatement is often on the mark.

"It sure holds the heat well."—Mets manager Casey Stengel talking about Busch Stadium after the 1966 All-Star Game

Not playing like a rookie

When he led the Cardinals in all three Triple Crown categories in his rookie season in 2000, hitting .328 with 37 homers and 130 RBI, Albert Pujols became the first Cardinal to win the team's Triple Crown since Ted Simmons in 1973.

Enthusiasm is contagious.

"When Ol' Diz was out there pitching, it was more than just another ballgame. It was a regular three-ring circus and everybody was wide awake and enjoying being alive."—Pepper Martin talking about Dizzy Dean

Don't waste time at work.

"Bob Gibson pitches as though he's
double parked."—Vin Scully

Some people just have it.

"Stan Musial could have hit .300 with
a fountain pen."—Joe Garagiola

Be able to laugh at your limitations.

"I've had pretty good success with Stan Musial,
by throwing him my best pitch and backing
up third."—Dodgers pitcher Carl Erskine

Take 'em any way
you can get 'em.

Tommy Thevenow hit two home runs for the Cardinals
in 1926, and both were inside-the-parkers. In the next
12 years of his career with the Cardinals and Pirates,
he never hit another homer.

(32)

It's never too early to do well.

Tim McCarver was only 17 years old when he made his major-league debut with the Cardinals in 1959. The future two-time All-Star played in eight games, batting .167.

Better Late than Never.

Barney Schultz was 37 years old and pitching in the minors
when he was summoned to the Cardinals on August 1, 1964.
He saved 14 games in the final two months of the year,
being instrumental in St. Louis winning the pennant.

Even Betty Crocker burns a cake once in a while.

Tommy Glaviano committed errors on three consecutive plays in the ninth inning of a May 18, 1950, game against Brooklyn, turning a would-be 8-5 win into a 9-8 defeat.

The total is what counts.

Lou Brock is one of 19 players in major-league history
to collect 3,000 hits in his career, but one of
only four who never won a league batting title.

They all add up.

Stan Musial is one of three major-league players
to hit more than 400 homers in his career but
never have a season in which he hit at least 40.
Musial's season-high was 39 in 1948.

One is better than none.

Future Hall-of-Fame manager Walter Alston played
in one game in his major-league career—for the Cardinals
on the final day of the 1936 season. He got his chance when
Johnny Mize was ejected, and Alston entered the game in
the seventh inning. In his only at-bat, Alston struck out.

Don't order an intentional walk just to keep your record intact.

When Jim Bottomley set the major-league record
of 12 RBI in one game on September 16, 1924,
it came against Brooklyn and broke the mark of
11 set by Wilson Robinson in 1892. The Dodgers
manager on that day in 1924? Robinson.

Comets are bright but brief.

Von McDaniel was 7-5 for the 1957 Cardinals as an 18-year-old direct out of high school, including a two-bit shutout over Brooklyn in his first major-league start. He pitched in two games in 1958, hurt his arm and saw his career over at age 19.

The first sometimes grows into the most.

The first of Hank Aaron's 755 career homers came against the Cardinals' Vic Raschi on April 23, 1954.

Try to exit on a positive note.

The 3,630th and final hit of Stan Musial's career
was a single on his last at-bat on September 29, 1963,
against the Reds' Jim Maloney. He was replaced by a
pinch-runner, Gary Kolb.

Don't trust the newspaper.

In reporting the trade of Ernie Broglio for Lou Brock in its
June 16, 1964, edition, the *St. Louis Post-Dispatch* said,
"Why didn't the Cardinals get more than Brock, a flashy
outfielder who could become a star, for Broglio, a 15-game
winner last season and still regarded as a top pitcher?"

Even when you have a great day, you may be overshadowed.

In his Cardinal debut June 16, 1964, Lou Brock batted second and had two hits, including a triple, and he stole one base. The star of the game was Ken Boyer, who hit for the cycle in the 7-1 win at Houston.

If at first you don't succeed, do more.

Rogers Hornsby lost the MVP race in 1924
despite leading the league with a .424 average.
He responded by winning the Triple Crown
in 1925, and did take home the MVP trophy.

When you spot a natural, let your bosses know.

After watching rookie Stan Musial play 12 games at the end of the 1941 season, during which he hit .426, manager Billy Southworth said, "That kid was born to play baseball."

The new standard

"The thing about Ozzie [Smith] is, if he misses a ball, you assume
it's uncatchable. If any other shortstop misses a ball,
your first thought is 'would Ozzie have had it?'"
—former New York Mets manager Bud Harrelson

Try, try again.

Al Hrabosky was cut from his Little League
team three years in a row and two consecutive
years from his junior high school team.

Knowledge is power.

"Your players have to respect your knowledge.
Be honest, be fair. But first, they have to know
that you know what the hell to do."—Whitey Herzog

Can't sleep?
Read the Rule Book.

"One paragraph on obstruction
and I'm asleep."—Whitey Herzog

Double the fun

The odds against it happening were probably impossible to
determine. On April 23, 1999, at Los Angeles, Fernando Tatis
became the first player in major league history to hit two
grand slams in one inning, and he hit both homers off
the same pitcher, the Dodgers' Chan Ho Park.

One is better than none.

The only Cardinal pitcher ever to win the Cy Young Award
was Bob Gibson who did it twice, in 1968 and 1970.

The fact that it has been done means it can be done.

No Cardinal has led the National League
in RBI since Joe Torre did it in 1971.

If you live by the long ball, you may die by it too.

The only Cardinal to hit more than 30 homers in a season since 1970 was Jack Clark, who hit 35 in 1987.

Ultimate respect

On May 24, 1998, Mark McGwire came to bat with two outs and
nobody on base in the 14th inning in a game against the San
Francisco Giants. Opposing manager Dusty Baker ordered
his pitcher to walk McGwire intentionally.

Swing hard from the start.

Two Cardinals have hit home runs in
their first at-bat in the major leagues—
Eddie Morgan in 1936 and Wally Moon in 1954.

Believe it; there is such a thing as a nemesis.

Between 1904 and 1909, the Cardinals faced Christy Mathewson of the Giants 25 times... and lost all 25 of those games. Twenty-four of the wins were credited to Mathewson.

That's the way the ball bounces.

The Cardinals lost a game to the Phillies in 1915
when a ball hit by George "Possum" Whitted hit off
the outfield wall, bounced back off Bob Boescher's
chest, and bounced back over the wall for a home run.

All losing streaks must end.

The Cardinals had lost 11 consecutive games in 1929
when they broke out of the slump with a 28-6 pounding
of the Phillies in the second game of a doubleheader. The
Cardinals scored 10 runs in each of two separate innings.

Save it 'til you really need it.

Carl Taylor's pinch-hit grand slam home run with two
outs in the bottom of the ninth inning capped a
five-run rally and gave the Cardinals an 11-10 victory
over San Diego on August 11, 1970. Taylor had never
hit a grand slam before, even in Little League.

Never give up.

In 1964 the Cardinals were six games out of first with
11 to play, but their hot finish and a collapse by the
Phillies allowed them to win their first pennant in
18 years on the season's final day.

Run out even the pop-ups; you never know...

A dropped pop-up by the Cubs allowed the
Cardinals to score in the ninth inning of their
September 13, 1964, game against Chicago,
becoming only the second NL team in history
to score at least one run in every inning.

Expect the unexpected.

The Cardinals should have known 1982
was going to be their year when third-string
catcher Glenn Brummer stole home with two outs
and two strikes on the hitter in the 12th inning,
giving St. Louis a win over the Giants on August 22.

No one has everything.

The only major career offensive categories in
which Stan Musial isn't the Cardinals' all-time
leader is in batting average and stolen bases.

Don't give up if you're not the first pick.

Keith Hernandez was the 42nd-round pick of the
Cardinals in 1971, the 783rd player selected in
the draft. The team's first-round choice that
year also was a first baseman, Ed Kurpiel.

Tomorrow will be a better day.

Richie Allen struck out five consecutive at-bats in
a game in 1970, one of 15 times in Allen's career that
he struck out at least four times in the same game.

Try to make the uncommon common.

For most players, one game in which they get
five hits is the highlight of their careers. In the
1948 season alone, Stan Musial did it four times.

Make a quick impression.

In his first two major-league games, in 1954,
Joe Cunningham hit three homers. He hit one in
his debut, then added two more the following day.

Real stars come through when the bases are loaded.

In his career, Stan Musial hit nine
grand slams…and added seven almost
grand slams, hitting seven bases-loaded triples.

The good ones can do it left-handed as well.

Three Cardinals—Red Schoendienst, Reggie Smith, and Ted Simmons—each hit home runs from both sides of the plate in one game.

Be the one they turn to with the game on the line.

For most players, hitting one pinch-hit grand slam would be one of the highlights of their careers, but not for Ron Northey. He played only three years for the Cardinals, 1947-49, but during that time hit two of his three career pinch-hit grand slams.

If you do the unexpected once, you can do it again.

Ed Konetchy had a game to remember on September 30, 1907.
He stole home twice in that game, two of the three steals of
home the Cardinals had on that one day.

Take it one hit at a time.

Only two Cardinals since 1900 have ever collected six hits in one game. Jim Bottomley did it twice, and Terry Moore once.

Silent debut

When he looks back at his major-league career, J. D. Drew will
have a couple of reasons to remember September 8, 1998,
when the Cardinals played the Cubs at Busch Stadium. It
marked his major league debut, which happened to also be
the same night Mark McGwire hit his 62nd home run,
breaking Roger Maris' home run record.

Nothing lasts forever.

The longest losing streak in Cardinals' history
is 14 consecutive games, in 1935.

Don't use it up in one year.

Ray Jablonski hit 21 homers for the Cardinals in 1953, which
still stands as the franchise's record. It also was the best year
of Jablonski's career…he never hit more than 15 again.

A Hall of Fame day

On the same day in January 2002 that he received the news that he had been elected to baseball's Hall of Fame, Ozzie Smith carried the Olympic torch through downtown St. Louis on its way to Salt Lake City, Utah, for the Winter Games.

When he was a student majoring in broadcasting at Ohio State University, one of Jack Buck's professors advised him, "I think you had better find something else to do for a living."

During his 50-plus years as a broadcaster, Buck was elected to 11 different Halls of Fame.

Try to see things from every angle.

"The difference between playing at home and on the road is that on the road, you can't go down to the kitchen to get a cup of coffee in the morning in your underwear."—Andy Van Slyke

Life may lead you to change sides.

During their playing careers, future Cardinal general manager Dal Maxvill and future manager Joe Torre served as the team's representatives to the player's union.

It is, in fact, all relative.

When they appeared together on the cover of
Sports Illustrated on October 7, 1968, as
"Baseball's Highest Paid Team," the combined
salaries of the Cardinals' nine starters and
manager Red Schoendienst was $607,000.

(81)

Nobody's perfect.

During his remarkable 1968 season, Bob Gibson pitched
a span of 92 innings in June and July in which he
allowed two runs, one of which scored on a wild pitch.

Practice makes perfect

When he was a young boy growing up in Los Angeles, Ozzie
Smith bounced balls off concrete steps, off the wall of his
house, anything he could think of. "I broke a few
windows, but it paid off," Smith said.

It doesn't matter where you play, only how well.

In 1979, Keith Hernandez became the first infielder to win a batting title and a Gold Glove in the same season. Not coincidentally, he shared the MVP award with Pittsburgh's Willie Stargell.

It's not over 'til it's over.

The Cardinals learned this adage on June 15, 1952,
in the first game of a doubleheader against the Giants
at the Polo Grounds. They were losing, 11-0, against
Sal Maglie after the third inning, but rallied to win,
14-12, equaling the biggest comeback in NL history.

Don't count your wins until you've won.

This lesson was driven into the Cardinals' minds
on July 18, 1994, playing in Houston. The Cardinals
were ahead, 11-0, after three innings, but saw the
Astros come back to win the game, 15-12.

Your contribution may ultimately lead to victory.

When Ken Reitz hit a two-out, two-strike homer in the ninth inning of the September 11, 1974, game in New York, all he knew was that it tied the game and sent it into extra innings. It was about five hours later, when they were still playing, that he knew what he had done. The Cardinals finally won the game, 4-3, in the 25th inning, the longest night game in NL history.

19 isn't always enough.

Steve Carlton pitched one of the best games of
his career on September 15, 1969, striking out a
then major-league record 19 Mets. It wasn't
enough to get him the victory, however, as he lost,
4-3, on a pair of two-run homers by Ron Swoboda.

Make the first hit a good one.

Roger Freed had not had a hit in the 1979 season
until May 1, when he came up to pinch-hit with
the bases loaded and two outs in the 11th inning of
a game against the Astros. With two strikes, Freed
slammed a grand slam that brought the Cardinals
from a three-run deficit to a 7-6 victory.

Go crazy, folks.

One of the most dramatic calls in broadcasting history
came when Jack Buck implored Cardinal fans to
"Go Crazy, Folks" after Ozzie Smith's ninth-inning
homer in the fifth game of the 1985 playoffs against the
Dodgers put St. Louis one win away from the World Series.

Hindsight bats 1,000.

Instead of pitching to Jack Clark with first base
open and runners on second and third in the ninth
inning of game six of the 1985 playoffs, the
Dodgers could have walked him. That would have
brought Andy Van Slyke to the plate, and would
have denied Clark perhaps one of the most memorable
homers in Cardinals' history, a three-run blast that
sent the team into the World Series.

Sometimes a mistake can rob you of your place in history.

Brian Harper would have been long remembered by Cardinals fans for getting the hit that won the 1985 World Series. Harper's piece of fame and glory was wiped out by a umpire's bad call, however, and the Royals won that game and won the World Series the next night in game seven.

Some things defy explanation.

It was seven years after Jackie Robinson's debut that the Cardinals finally fielded a black player on April 13, 1954. He was first baseman Tom Alston.

Go for the record wherever they put you.

Stan Musial holds the single-season record
for most home runs by all three outfield
positions—32 as a left fielder in 1951,
21 as a center fielder in 1952, and
39 as a right fielder in 1948.

When a homer isn't a homer

Mike Matheny lost a home run in spring training 2002 when he batted out of turn. The last time that happened in a regular-season game was on June 29, 1933, when Ethan Allen of the Cardinals hit an inside-the-park homer at the Polo Grounds but was called out for batting out of order. He did not hit another homer that year.

When you have it, use it.

In his great career, Lou Brock stole two bases in the
same game 135 times. He stole three bases in a game
19 times and his career high of four steals was
accomplished on three occasions.

You can be undefeated for three years and still be forgotten.

Ted Wilks made 77 consecutive appearances between September 8, 1945, and April 29, 1948, and managed to do something rather remarkable. Not once in that span did he lose a game. All but four of his appearances were in relief, and his record during the streak was 12-0.

You don't have to clear the wall to circle the bases.

Ken Boyer wasn't the fastest player ever to play for the Cardinals, but he did something not many players have accomplished. In a three-week span in 1959, Boyer hit three inside-the-park home runs.

If you're in the lineup every day, you don't get many chances to pinch-hit.

Stan Musial holds the Cardinals' career record
with 475 homers, but only two of them
came as a pinch-hitter—on May 12, 1951,
and September 26, 1962.

One is better than none.

There have been 64 players in history whose
entire Cardinal career has lasted one game.
The most recent member added to the club
was pitcher Barry Lersch in 1974.

If your name is Slim, you'd better know how to slide.

The only Cardinal pitcher in history to
steal home in a game was Slim Sallee on
July 22, 1913, against the New York Giants.

The final word.

Pitcher Joaquin Andujar was a philosopher
when he wasn't performing on the mound,
and he said that everything about baseball
could be summed up in one word—Youneverknow.